# STAR WARS™

# BB-8

## AN INSIDE LOOK AT
## THE INTREPID LITTLE ASTROMECH DROID

WRITTEN BY DANIEL WALLACE

INCREDI BUILDS

*a division of*
INSIGHT EDITIONS

*San Rafael, California*

# INTRODUCTION

**He can roll in any direction, but every path seems to lead straight into trouble.**

**He carries an entire toolbox, but none of it is visible outside his roly-poly body.**

**He can't speak, yet his whistles, beeps, and murmurs carry plenty of meaning.**

He's BB-8—the breakout star of *Star Wars: The Force Awakens*, and the most adorable droid to appear in a *Star Wars* movie since R2-D2 wheeled on screen way back in 1977.

Fans started buzzing about BB-8 even before the movie. When the droid first popped up in the teaser trailer for *The Force Awakens*, the questions began. *How does he move, exactly? Does that dome always stay upright?* And, most importantly, would audiences warm up to an unfamiliar new droid sidekick?

The answer to that last question, at least, was a resounding *yes*. Not only did BB-8 wow viewers with his technical sophistication—the sight of a full-sized BB-8 on stage at 2015's *Star Wars* Celebration amazed onlookers—but he also displayed a winning personality: endearingly shy and stubbornly outspoken at the same time.

In *The Force Awakens* and *Star Wars: The Last Jedi*, BB-8 is a worthy champion of the Resistance, and comics and books have added even more achievements to his service record. BB-8 is the unofficial fourth member of the Rey-Finn-Poe team, loyal and brave in equal measure.

Whatever happens in future clashes between the Resistance and the First Order, one thing is clear: BB-8 is sure to be in the thick of the action.

# MEET BB-8

BB-8 is a BB-series astromech droid—one of thousands of near-identical models manufactured to help pilots operate their spacecraft. But BB-8, of course, could never be replaced by a generic factory model.

Thanks to a unique personality and a string of incredible adventures, BB-8 is a special, irreplaceable droid. His owner, Poe Dameron, considers BB-8 a true friend.

## TECHNICAL SPECIFICATIONS

**FUNCTION:** Astromech droid

**HEIGHT:** 0.67 meters

**WEIGHT:** 18 kilograms

**BODY COLOR**: White

**TRIM COLOR:** Orange

**METHOD OF LOCOMOTION:** Rolling body with free-moving, domed head

**TOOLS AND ACCESSORIES:** Cable launchers, electrical arc welder, welding torch, holoprojector

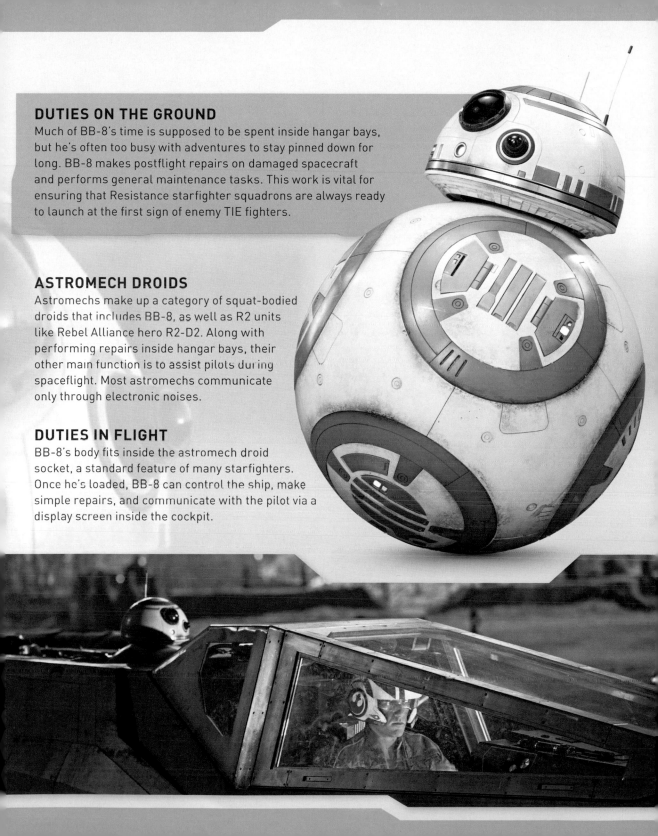

### DUTIES ON THE GROUND

Much of BB-8's time is supposed to be spent inside hangar bays, but he's often too busy with adventures to stay pinned down for long. BB-8 makes postflight repairs on damaged spacecraft and performs general maintenance tasks. This work is vital for ensuring that Resistance starfighter squadrons are always ready to launch at the first sign of enemy TIE fighters.

### ASTROMECH DROIDS

Astromechs make up a category of squat-bodied droids that includes BB-8, as well as R2 units like Rebel Alliance hero R2-D2. Along with performing repairs inside hangar bays, their other main function is to assist pilots during spaceflight. Most astromechs communicate only through electronic noises.

### DUTIES IN FLIGHT

BB-8's body fits inside the astromech droid socket, a standard feature of many starfighters. Once he's loaded, BB-8 can control the ship, make simple repairs, and communicate with the pilot via a display screen inside the cockpit.

# FULL OF SURPRISES

The orange-and-white checkerboard design of BB-8's body isn't merely decoration: Each panel conceals a hidden compartment. Some of these are packed with specialized tools or even just space for stashing important items and secret treasures.

## WELDING TORCH

This basic tool is a mainstay among astromech droids. BB-8's welding torch uses a small flame to cut through metal sheets or make a molten bond between two surfaces.

## CABLE LAUNCHERS

High-pressure launchers are spaced equidistantly around BB-8's spherical body so he can fire cables from any direction. The tips of these cables can affix to any surface, allowing BB-8 to reel himself up and over obstacles or yank distant objects into his grasp. By deploying multiple cables at once, BB-8 can keep himself in place in the event of severe starship turbulence.

## ELECTRICAL ARC WELDER

This tool uses an electrical spark to perform precise welding, but it can also deliver a nasty shock. BB-8 sometimes uses his electrical arc welder to keep enemies at a safe distance.

## STARFIGHTER PLUG-IN ARMS

A lot of BB-8's hardware is designed to interface with X-wings and similar military-grade starfighters. BB-8 deploys these mechanical probes only after he has been loaded into his astromech socket. By linking with the ship's systems, BB-8 can communicate with the hyperdrive engine and operate the flight controls by himself.

## STORAGE COMPARTMENTS

Several of BB-8's panels slide open to reveal empty spaces beneath. These compartments are big enough to carry small items such as spare tools and data tapes. Poe Dameron used BB-8's compartments to conceal a star map he received on Jakku from agents of the First Order.

# ASTROMECHS ASSEMBLE

BB-8 isn't the only astromech droid who pitches in to fix starships and maintain equipment. Some astromech droids are even used by the First Order!

**BB-4:** This droid belongs to the same BB series as BB-8 himself but can be differentiated from the other Resistance astromechs by his tan coloration.

**R4-X2:** This vintage droid has been in service since the days of the Rebel Alliance, as evidenced by the classic rebel sigil on her cranial assembly. She still serves faithfully aboard the main Resistance cruiser.

**2BB-2:** Designated with a catchy name, this blue-gray BB-series astromech droid is frequently found in Resistance starfighter hangars.

**Y5-X2:** This astromech shares repair duties with R4-X2 aboard the primary Resistance cruiser, but he came off the assembly line more recently. Y5 works extra hard in the hope of impressing others with his tireless service.

**BB-9E:** One of the astromech droids employed by the First Order to maintain its military equipment, BB-9E has a glossy black exterior and sports the latest technological advances.

# A PILOT'S BEST FRIEND

Like all astromech droids, BB-8 is designed to serve as an autonomous plug-in for military starfighters and other interstellar craft. BB-8 has long been the droid partner of Resistance pilot Poe Dameron, providing in-flight assistance for Poe's personal X-wing starfighter, *Black One*.

## POE DAMERON

Poe Dameron, leader of the Resistance's top starfighter squadron and BB-8's piloting partner, has adventure in his blood. His mother flew an A-wing during the Battle of Endor, and his father served as a groundside commando during the same conflict. Poe followed in his mother's footsteps by becoming a pilot for the New Republic, but both he and BB-8 grew disillusioned with the government's lack of concern for the growing threat of the First Order. When the opportunity presented itself, he jumped ship to join General Leia Organa's Resistance movement and brought BB-8 with him.

Flying under the call sign "Black Leader," Poe formed Black Squadron out of the Resistance's best pilots. BB-8 forged bonds with the squadron's other astromech droids and helped Poe's team escape deadly danger on many occasions. Poe's hotshot antics aren't always popular with Resistance commanders, but after the Battle of Starkiller Base, Poe was promoted to the rank of captain.

## BLACK ONE

BB-8's and Poe Dameron's preferred ship is a T-70 X-wing fighter, armed with four laser cannons, each at the end of the ship's four wingtips, and a pair of proton torpedo launchers built into the fuselage. A rotating light blaster cannon can deploy from the starfighter's underside, providing an unwelcome surprise for any First Order stormtroopers. The most recent addition to the ship is a boosted accelerator pod, which provides extra speed for quick escapes.

When BB-8 is plugged into *Black One*'s astromech socket, he can control almost every aspect of the ship. His primary duties involve calculating hyperspace coordinates and sending them to the hyperdrive engine, as well as finding ways to boost the X-wing's in-flight performance. BB-8 can do a lot more than that, if necessary. He can even fly *Black One* solo if Poe is unable to take his usual place in the cockpit.

# TRUSTED ALLIES, TREACHEROUS FOES

BB-8 has a knack for getting into trouble. This habit has won him a number of steadfast friends but has also attracted attention from some of the galaxy's vilest villains.

### REY
This desert scavenger from Jakku lived inside an abandoned AT-AT walker until she rescued BB-8 from Teedo, a fellow junker. Rey took a liking to the little orange droid and helped him escape the clutches of unscrupulous junk dealer Unkar Plutt.

### FINN
After he defected from the First Order's stormtrooper corps, Finn tried to pass himself off as a member of the Resistance. Finn looked to BB-8 for help in maintaining his ruse and keeping the truth from their traveling companion, Rey. BB-8 reluctantly played along, aiding Finn while arranging for his own return to Poe Dameron at the Resistance base on D'Qar. Later, BB-8 joined Finn and new ally Rose on an adventure to help the Resistance.

### HAN SOLO AND CHEWBACCA
The famous Corellian smuggler and his Wookiee copilot had been flying the hyperspace lanes for decades when they encountered BB-8 and his friends aboard their former ship, the *Millennium Falcon*. When some of Han's former business associates tried to claim the bounty on BB-8, the smugglers helped protect the little droid and see him safely back to the Resistance.

## R2-D2 AND C-3PO

When BB-8 encountered an inactive R2-D2, he tried to wake up the older astromech. A short time later, a rejuvenated R2-D2 returned to active duty with the Resistance. Both R2-D2 and C-3PO are legends of the Rebel Alliance and proof that droids can be heroes too.

## ROSE

This no-nonsense member of the Resistance is part of the support crew that keeps the X-wings and other starfighters in top condition. Rose, who has hated the First Order since she was a girl, embarks on a new adventure to strike back at her enemies when she joins Finn and BB-8 on a dangerous mission.

## KYLO REN

As the First Order's most powerful enforcer, Kylo Ren led the stormtrooper mission to wipe out a Jakku village while on the hunt for a valuable star map. After Kylo Ren learned that a droid might be carrying the secret data, he had his First Order agents issue an alert. Soon, every crook in the galaxy was on BB-8's trail.

## UNKAR PLUTT

Unkar Plutt, a rubbery-skinned Crolute, ran a trading outpost on Jakku. He was one of the first people to realize that BB-8 might fetch a high price from the right buyer. When Rey refused his offer to purchase the droid, Unkar Plutt ordered his thugs to steal BB-8 instead.

## KANJIKLUB AND RATHTARS

BB-8 escaped Jakku with Rey and Finn aboard the *Millennium Falcon*. For a moment, it looked like his troubles might be over. But that was before the criminals of Kanjiklub caught up with them and decided to claim the reward for BB-8's capture. Things got even worse when a cargo of hungry rathtars escaped from the holding cells of Han Solo's heavy freighter, the *Eravana*, and ran wild through the corridors.

# INTERGALACTIC ADVENTURER

BB-8's adventures have taken him from one side of the galaxy to the other as he helps the Resistance in putting down the threat of the First Order once and for all.

## TAKODANA

A lush world of lakes and forests, Takodana is the site of a castle fortress operated by Maz Kanata, which acts as a neutral meeting ground for pirates and smugglers. BB-8 arrives on Takodana aboard the *Millennium Falcon* but is forced to flee when the First Order attacks.

## D'QAR

This jungle planet, home to the Resistance's secret headquarters, is circled by spectacular rings of rock and ice. BB-8 returns to D'Qar to reunite with Poe Dameron and prepare for the assault against the First Order's ultimate weapon.

## JAKKU

This desert planet was once the site of a battle between the Empire and the New Republic. BB-8 survived in the sun-baked wastelands after becoming separated from Poe Dameron, and he made new friends in Rey and Finn.

## STARKILLER BASE

The First Order hollowed out the core of this snowy world in the Unknown Regions to create a super-weapon capable of destroying entire star systems. BB-8 and Poe fly their X-wing fighter through the base's defenses, hoping to strike a death blow against the fearsome weapon.

# TIGHT SCRAPES

Thanks to his array of clever tools and his never-say-die attitude, BB-8 has rolled, fixed, and charmed his way through a lifetime of adventures.

## PERSUASION

After Rey frees him from a scavenger's net on Jakku, BB-8 uses his most endearing hums and whistles to convince his new friend to help him in his quest.

## ZAP!

Using his electrical arc welder, BB-8 shocks Finn, fearful that the human is a First Order agent.

## THUMBS UP

When Finn tries to convince Rey that he is a member of the Resistance, BB-8 encourages his new friend with an optimistic gesture, formed by igniting the flame of his arc welder.

## ON DISPLAY

BB-8's holoprojector has many uses. On D'Qar, he shows an audience of Resistance leaders how a piece of a holographic star map fits into the larger whole.

# EXPANDED ADVENTURES

BB-8's heroics aren't confined to the movie screen. Comic books such as the monthly series *Star Wars: Poe Dameron* have filled out BB-8's backstory, while novels, illustrated storybooks, and an animated micro-series offer new perspectives on the Resistance's pint-sized operative.

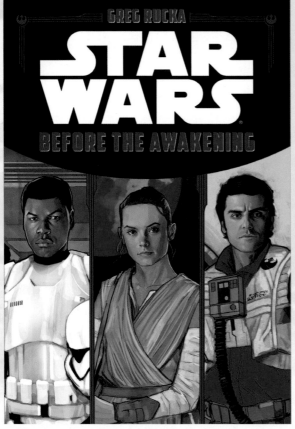

## BEGINNINGS

Greg Rucka's novel *Before the Awakening* pulls back the curtain to reveal how Poe Dameron and BB-8 joined the Resistance in the first place. In this tale, Poe and his droid companion are flying with the New Republic's Rapier Squadron when they witness First Order ships attack a freighter. When Poe's superiors refuse to take the threat seriously, Poe and BB-8 depart on their own mission and reveal the existence of a deadly First Order fleet. General Leia Organa soon offers Poe the chance to fly for her forces, and Poe and BB-8 become the newest Resistance recruits.

## MATCHMAKER

In "Sabotage," a short comics story by Chris Eliopoulos, BB-8 plays Cupid to unite a lovesick Resistance mechanic with a preoccupied X-wing pilot. BB-8's well-meaning acts of starfighter sabotage cause plenty of headaches for everyone in the hangar, but they result in a successful love connection just the same.

## ON THE HUNT

In Poe Dameron's comic book series, General Leia Organa orders her top pilot to locate Lor San Tekka as the first step in pinning down the whereabouts of her brother, Luke Skywalker. When the trail leads Black Squadron to the maximum-security prison Megalox, BB-8 foils a surprise double-cross by rallying his fellow astromech droids and shutting down the prison's gravitational safeguards. The warden sends a security bot to destroy them, but BB-8 turns the tables with his cable launchers and his electricity-zapping arc welder.

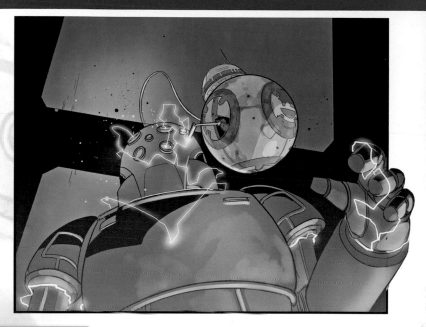

## MENACED BY TEEDO

In *Star Wars: The Force Awakens*, BB-8 is seen in the possession of a desert scavenger named Teedo before Rey is able to secure his release. The book *BB-8 on the Run* explores how BB-8 ends up in such a predicament, revealing that the good-hearted droid tried to save Teedo from a sinkhole only to learn that he'd been tricked. With help from a loading droid named Fez, BB-8 nearly escapes Jakku aboard Fez's ship—but allows himself to fall back into Teedo's clutches in order to give his friend a clean shot at freedom.

## TEEDO AND THE NIGHTWATCHER

After Rey frees BB-8 from Teedo, the two of them run into a nightwatcher worm in the animated micro-series *Star Wars: Forces of Destiny*. Though they outwit the metal-eating monster, they apply the lessons from their encounter the following day when Teedo tries to reclaim his property. By tricking Teedo into an ambush, they lure a nightwatcher into hungrily devouring their rival's speeder. Now safe from pursuit, Rey and BB-8 race off in the direction of Niima Outpost.

# GALAXY OF FUN

BB-8 is cute, charismatic, and technologically innovative. This winning combination has led to a dizzying variety of tie-in merchandise, ranging from the familiar to the revolutionary.

### REMOTE-CONTROLLED ROLLING BB-8

A rolling ball droid with an auto-balancing head seemed like science fiction when the trailer for *The Force Awakens* dropped in theaters. So when news broke that a toy company had successfully built a miniature consumer model, the Sphero app-enabled BB-8 became a must-have for the 2015 holiday season.

### BB-8 IN BRICK

One of the most entertaining byproducts of the partnership between LEGO and *Star Wars* is the opportunity to see the saga's heroes and villains immortalized in plastic as tiny minifigures. BB-8 is no exception, with his minifig a prominent inclusion in LEGO sets like Encounter on Jakku and Resistance X-wing fighter. The little droid also pops up in "Poe to the Rescue," an animated short that is part of the larger adventure *LEGO Star Wars: The Resistance Rises*.

### NICE AND SMOOTH

BB-8 becomes a pump-action lotion dispenser in this mash-up of traditional housewares items and robot designs from a galaxy far, far away.

## HEAD TOPPER

BB-8's dome is an iconic part of his look, so what better clothing item to capture his essence than a knit beanie cap? There's even a pom-pom on top for maximum winter style points.

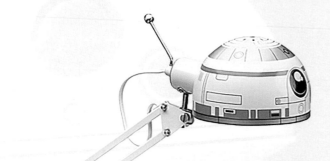

## BRIGHT IDEA

This classic desktop lamp is the perfect shape for a pleasing BB-8 interpretation.

## STAR SOCKS

One of the advantages of BB-8's design is that he can be evoked with only a handful of features and colors. These socks are a perfect example of the principle—they don't share BB-8's shape, but they're indisputably BB-8 nonetheless.

## RECHARGE YOUR POWER CELLS

Need a jolt of java? BB-8 is your companion every morning when you take your coffee swigs out of this faithfully detailed ceramic mug.

# BEHIND THE SCENES

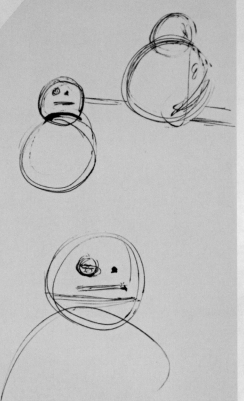

BB-8 began with a sketch, a simple doodle drawn by *The Force Awakens* director J. J. Abrams (left). Two circles and a dot for an eye were enough to suggest the form for the movie's droid star. Though influenced by the iconic robot R2-D2, BB-8 would incorporate a groundbreaking new method of locomotion and become an icon for a new era of *Star Wars*.

Concept designer Christian Alzmann worked to flesh out Abrams's initial sketch. From there, another concept designer, Jake Lunt Davies, took a crack (below). They both experimented with various configurations for BB-8's body shapes and facial features, looking for the perfect arrangement that could convey a range of emotion.

Neal Scanlan, head of the creature shop for *The Force Awakens*, took on the challenge of bringing BB-8 to life and ultimately decided to build the droid in many different configurations that could each be used for specific shots in the film. "The design already existed as a hemisphere on a ball, so our challenge was bringing this to the screen," Scanlan told StarWars. com. "The idea of having versions of BB-8, which we knew we could have aspects digitally removed, opened up a much greater sphere of possibility."

This meant that BB-8 could be realized on set through multiple methods, with each design suited for a particular filming need—from puppeteering to remote-operated rolling. Senior animatronic designer Joshua Lee crafted a puppet BB-8 as a proof-of-concept model. "I built, in half a day, a little polystyrene puppet with the main movements," he said. "All the head movements and the ball rolling around, and handles on the back. It was just so expressive. You could see that there weren't any other fancy movements needed, that there's so much expression and character actually in the shapes and in the way the head sort of arched over the sphere."

A full-sized puppet BB-8 would ultimately be constructed for *The Force Awakens*. To create a performance using this creation, puppeteers Dave Chapman and Brian Herring needed to understand how BB-8 would react to moments of danger or elation. "We had, I guess, two weeks to ourselves on an empty soundstage, just figuring out how this character moved," said Chapman.

Added Herring, "BB-8 can cock his head over and look away, he can double take, he can look scared, he can look angry. We managed to find a whole vocabulary of movement for him."

When the creature shop showed its BB-8 to J. J. Abrams, the director responded with enthusiastic relief. The crew set to work building a legion of specialized droids. These included the "wiggler" for close-up shots of twisting and turning, "trikes" that had stabilizer wheels for smooth remote operation, a model that could be safely handled by the actors during filming, and a "bowling ball" that remained upright when tossed into a shot.

Because the crew had a BB-8 for every occasion, an all-purpose remote control BB-8 wasn't needed during filming. But as a special treat for the *Star Wars* Celebration fan convention, a fully emotive, free-rolling BB-8 was created by Joshua Lee, with software by Matthew Denton and exterior detailing by Henrik Svensson. This BB-8 debuted to rave reviews in April 2015.

## SAY ANYTHING

Comedians Bill Hader and Ben Schwartz (right) provided the backing vocalizations for BB-8's distinctive style of speaking. Post-production digital effects and electronic distortions further obscured the original recordings.

## WHAT'S IN A NAME?

Director J. J. Abrams gave BB-8 his memorable moniker. "I named him BB-8 because it was almost onomatopoeia," he told *Entertainment Weekly*. "It was sort of how he looked to me, with the 8, obviously, and then the two Bs."

## PRACTICALITY

The droid's ball-shaped body, a necessity for his chosen mode of transportation, offered a number of opportunities for variation and surprise. His colored surface panels helped convey a sense of rolling movement to the viewer, while ensuring that the compartments had a practical, believable function.

## GENDER

Whether a droid is coded male or female has always been one of the less-obvious aspects of *Star Wars* roboticism. In BB-8's case, the droid started out as female according to some designers, including Neal Scanlan. "BB-8 was female in our eyes," he said. "And then he or she became male. And that's all part of the evolution, not only visually, but in the way they move, how they hold themselves."

# INTERVIEW

Concept artist Christian Alzmann helped define BB-8's look during the character's early evolution. Alzmann, who first saw *Star Wars: A New Hope* at the age of five, credits the space saga with inspiring his love of drawing. After graduating from Pasadena's ArtCenter College of Design—chosen because legendary *Star Wars* artist Ralph McQuarrie had attended the same school—Alzmann started working for Industrial Light & Magic (ILM). Now an eighteen-year ILM veteran, Alzmann worked on a number of character design concepts for *The Force Awakens*, including BB-8.

**WHAT DIRECTION WERE YOU GIVEN TO START WITH? AS I UNDERSTAND IT, THE EARLIEST BB-8 SKETCH CAME FROM J. J. ABRAMS.**

Yes. We had a few designs for BB-8 prior to that, but nothing was quite sticking with J. J. He sent along a Post-it note drawing that looked like a snowman without a chest, just two spheres. It was enough to go on. I did eight to ten designs after that to hone in on where we ended up.

**AT THE TIME, DID YOU REALIZE HOW IMPORTANT BB-8 WOULD BE AS A CHARACTER?**

No, it was more like, "There's going to be this little sidekick droid. Do you want to take a pass on it?" I really didn't think it was going to be a big deal; [I thought] it would be in one scene or something. We knew he might have some plans he was carrying, but I didn't think he was going to be the next R2-D2.

**FROM THE EARLY SKETCH, YOU OBVIOUSLY KNEW BB-8 WOULD HAVE A ROLLING BODY AND AN UPRIGHT HEAD. HOW CONCERNED WERE YOU ABOUT WHETHER SUCH A CONFIGURATION COULD ACTUALLY BE BUILT IN REAL LIFE?**

As concept artists, we don't have to concern ourselves exactly with how something will work—but we have to make it look like it *could* work. If it isn't believable, the audience is going to check out. Once I realized it would be rolling and that the head would almost have to hover, I was thinking of computer graphics. With computer graphics now, we can do hard-surfaced things so well that I don't think anyone can tell. But when I saw the rod-controlled puppet version of it, and the remote-controlled one that they rolled out on stage at *Star Wars* Celebration, I was like, "Holy cow!" I had no clue.

**HOW CLOSELY DID YOU FEEL YOU NEEDED TO MAKE BB-8 RESEMBLE R2-D2 AND OTHER DROIDS LIKE HIM FROM THE FILMS?**

J. J. really liked the familiarity of *A New Hope*, so for the top of the head, I definitely was pushing toward an astromech droid design. The ring around the top of the head, the one big eye, the projector nozzle, I tried to get all of that stuff in there. The overall design was enough of a departure that I felt like we could have all that stuff and make it feel like *Star Wars*.

DROID REPAIR AREA VIEW I

### HOW ABOUT BB-8'S BALL BODY? DID YOU KNOW RIGHT AWAY HOW HE WOULD MOVE?

For the bottom—the "drive ball," as I always called it—we were initially going for it having a bunch of surfaces like typewriter keys that could extend out and help it move across different surfaces by giving it traction, like a knobby tire. They could extend or be flat to the surface, so it could be bumpy or smooth. We worked on that for a while, but J. J.'s decision was that *Star Wars* needs to be a quick read. You don't need to think about how R2-D2 is able to go on a sand dune.

### AND THE BODY WOULD NEED TO CONTAIN TOOLS AND ARMS FOR GRABBING THINGS, CORRECT?

Yes, we were thinking it would be like R2's body with all sorts of hidden compartments. And so [I tried] to figure out how to design a sphere and how to break it up visually. When you're working on a project like that you end up looking at everything spherical around you in your everyday life, and I realized that people that design soccer balls basically design spheres for a living. I looked at a lot of things like that to figure out how to break up the pattern. For a while, in fact, we called BB-8 the soccer-ball droid.

### WHAT HAPPENED TO YOUR DESIGNS ONCE YOU FINISHED THEM? MORE CONCEPT DESIGN WORK BEFORE IT WENT TO THE CREATURE SHOP?

I got the ball rolling, pardon the pun, but then I was whisked away to work on set design. It went to Jake [Lunt Davies] and others to figure out the final patterning and detailing. And I loved what those guys did with it—they pushed more toward seeing a face on the head and I loved that they made it a little abstract. You can sort of read a face there, but you don't see one.

### SO ONCE THE CREATURE SHOP STARTED CONSTRUCTING PHYSICAL VERSIONS OF BB-8 FOR FILMING, IT WAS A WHILE BEFORE YOU SAW WHAT THEY'D BUILT, CORRECT?

Yes, you just go on to the next project, and in my case I started designing interiors for a space on Jakku where we might meet BB-8. I don't think I saw him again for at least a few months. I knew the design went over well and they were building it, but there's always a euphoric moment when you actually see a physical version of something you've designed.

### DID YOU EVER HAVE A MOMENT OF PANIC, LIKE, "I HOPE PEOPLE DON'T GET ANGRY AND THINK WE'RE TRYING TO REPLACE R2-D2!"

I thought, "How do we know? This could be a hated character!" I mean I was happy with the design and happy with the way he could move, but sometimes in a movie it doesn't work out. I was nervous, and I had no idea that the next time I went to Disneyland I would be surrounded by sweatshirts, mugs, and toys with BB-8 on them.

# MAKE IT YOUR OWN

One of the great things about IncrediBuilds™ models is that each one is completely customizable. The untreated natural wood can be decorated with paints, pencils, pens, beads, sequins—the list goes on and on!

Before you start building and decorating your model, choose a theme and make a plan. You can create a replica of the adorable astromech droid BB-8, or you can make something completely different. Anything goes! Read through this sample project to get you started and those creative juices flowing.

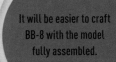

It will be easier to craft BB-8 with the model fully assembled.

## WHAT YOU NEED:

• Paints (white, orange, silver, black, red, and blue)
• Paintbrush

## WHAT YOU MIGHT WANT:

• Brown watercolor paint
• Fine detail brush

1. Paint the assembled model white. Let dry.

2. Paint the orange and silver details by following the engraved lines.

3. Paint the optical lenses black and let dry.

4. Add highlights to the optical lenses and paint a red dot for the red glow.

**TIP:** If the red paint doesn't show up on the black, paint a dot of white first, and then add the red on top of the white.

5. Add small blue lights as desired.

## GO A STEP FURTHER

To add some wear to BB-8, take brown watercolor paint and make it extra watery. Paint it around the edges of the white. It will pool in the engraved lines. When it dries, use a slightly damp paintbrush to soften the edges of the color or move it around to where you like.  Be careful to store your model away from water—if it gets wet at all, the paint effect will be destroyed.

IncrediBuilds™
A Division of Insight Editions LP
PO Box 3088
San Rafael, CA 94912
www.insighteditions.com
www.incredibuilds.com

Find us on Facebook: www.facebook.com/InsightEditions
Follow us on Twitter: @insighteditions

Library of Congress Cataloging-in-Publication Data available.

ISBN: 978-1-68298-087-3

Publisher: Raoul Goff
Associate Publisher: Jon Goodspeed
Art Director: Chrissy Kwasnik
Designers: Yousef Ghorabni and Alison Corn
Senior Editor: Chris Prince
Managing Editor: Alan Kaplan
Editorial Assistant: Holly Fisher
Production Editor: Carly Chillmon
Associate Production Manager: Sam Taylor
Product Development Manager: Rebekah Piatte
Model Designer: He Jianzhu, TeamGreen

For Lucasfilm:
Assistant Editor: Samantha Holland
Senior Editor: Frank Parisi
Creative Director of Publishing: Michael Siglain
Art Director: Troy Alders
Story Group: James Waugh, Pablo Hidalgo, Leland Chee
Image Unit: Steve Newman, Newell Todd, Gabrielle Levenson, Erik Sanchez, Bryce Pinkos, Tim Mapp, and Nicole Lacoursiere

MANUFACTURED IN CHINA

10 9 8 7 6 5 4 3 2

ROOTS of PEACE    REPLANTED PAPER

Insight Editions, in association with Roots of Peace, will plant two trees for each tree used in the manufacturing of this book. Roots of Peace is an internationally renowned humanitarian organization dedicated to eradicating land mines worldwide and converting war-torn lands into productive farms and wildlife habitats. Roots of Peace will plant two million fruit and nut trees in Afghanistan and provide farmers there with the skills and support necessary for sustainable land use.

Images on pages 20–21 are courtesy of RanchoObiWan.org. Rancho Obi-Wan is a nonprofit museum in Northern California that is home to the Guinness World Records' largest collection of *Star Wars* memorabilia, owned by author and collector Steve Sansweet. For information about membership and tours, go to RanchoObiWan.org.

Insight Editions would like to thank Leland Chee, Pablo Hidalgo, Samantha Holland, Daniel Saeva, Angela Ontiveros, Steve Sansweet, and Krista Wong.

## ABOUT THE AUTHOR

**DANIEL WALLACE** is the author or coauthor of more than two dozen books, including *The Joker*, *The Jedi Path*, *Man of Steel: Inside the Legendary World of Superman*, *DC Comics Year by Year*, *The Marvel Encyclopedia*, and the *New York Times* best-selling *Star Wars: The New Essential Guide to Characters*.